D0742385

Hoaxes

by Judith Herbst

Lerner Publications Company • Minneapolis

Lerner Publications Company
A division of Lerner Publishing Group
241 First Avenue North
Minneapolis, Minnesota 55401 U.S.A.

Website address: www.lernerbooks.com

Library of Congress Cataloging-in-Publication Data

Herbst, Judith.
    Hoaxes / by Judith Herbst.
        p.   cm. — (The unexplained)
    Summary: A look at some of history's most famous hoaxes and publicity stunts,
    including fairy photographs, moon-men, lost tribes, and crop circles.
    Includes index.
    ISBN: 0–8225–1629–2 (lib. bdg. : alk. paper)
    1. Occultism. 2. Impostors and imposture. 3. Curiosities and wonders.
    [1. Occultism. 2. Imposters and imposture. 3. Curiosities and wonders.] I. Title.
    II. Series: Unexplained (Lerner Publications)
    BF1042.H44 2005
    001.9'5—dc22   2003022692

Manufactured in the United States of America
1 2 3 4 5 6 – JR – 10 09 08 07 06 05

There's a sucker born every minute.

—P. T. Barnum

4

CHAPTER 1

SHERLOCK HOLMES GETS FLIMFLAMMED

Our first story is a fairy tale. It begins in England.

It is the merry month of May 1917. Sir Arthur Conan Doyle, creator of the great fictional detective Sherlock Holmes, receives a letter from a friend. Actual photographs, says the letter, have been taken of fairies and gnomes. Doyle gasps. He has been enchanted by this subject for quite some time and could not be more delighted by the news. Ever since he became convinced that the dead can communicate with the living, he has been a regular at séances. Now it seems that fairies are real. His eyes twinkle, and he immediately hires Edward Gardner to investigate. He should have hired Holmes.

Edward Gardner is a follower of a strange little religion called theosophy. Theosophy is a mystical open house for ghosts, pixies, and all things wacko. So asking Gardner to check out the fairy photographs is like sending a termite into a lumberyard. Nevertheless, off he goes, and a short time later, Doyle gets a little package in the mail. It contains two photographs.

To us, these pictures look phonier than a chocolate quarter, mostly because the subject matter is rather suspect, but Doyle practically swoons.

FAIRIES

Fairies are said to be small, supernatural beings who live in an enchanted land. They are usually green, wear green clothing, and can make themselves invisible. Most fairies are gentle little things, but some are evil and should be avoided at all costs.

The concept of the fairy is quite old. Throughout the centuries, people have claimed fairy encounters. Usually these encounters take place in a dense forest, where people are walking alone at night. Fairies seem to be part of an alternate universe, a land of make-believe that we sometimes glimpse if we are lucky or in the right place at the right time.

Frances Griffiths (*above*) and Elsie Wright (*right*) pose with their fairy friends.

Gardner's enclosed letter has informed Doyle that the photographers are 10-year-old Frances Griffiths and her 16-year-old cousin, Elsie Wright.

The camera they used was a Midg Quarter that exposed the image onto a glass plate (instead of film). The exposure time (how long the camera lens stays open to record the image) was 1/50th of a second. Modern cameras can take pictures much faster than that, but in those days, 1/50th of a second was considered, as Gardner described it, instantaneous. Elsie's father had loaded the camera, and the girls had taken it to Cottingley Glen, a little valley where they said they often played with fairies, pixies, and gnomes.

Well, Doyle is just bubbling, so he shows the pictures to his friend, Sir Oliver Lodge. Lodge is a respected physicist who

Be Careful What You Wish For

The best part of any séance is when the spirits of the deceased materialize out of thin air, helped along by a medium. In July 1960, two psychic researchers, Tom O'Neill and Andrija Puharich, tried to capture one of these spirit materializations on film. With the permission of medium Edith Stillwell, they brought an army night-vision scope and an infrared camera to one of Stillwell's séances.

The room was darkened, Stillwell went into her medium routine, O'Neill's camera rolled, and Puharich peered through his scope. But instead of ghosts, Puharich saw Stillwell's helpers, wearing white chiffon, sneak in through a hidden door. The film confirmed it. The spiritualists had unmasked themselves.

had started going to séances after the death of his youngest son. If anybody would be receptive to pictures of fairies, it would likely be Lodge. But despite his ghostly beliefs, Lodge is not impressed and expresses considerable doubt about the photos. Doyle, however, dismisses Lodge by insisting that the two little girls who took the pictures came from a very good family and would hardly have known how to fake the images.

Doyle then hands the pictures off to a professional photographer named Snelling, who studies them with great care. Snelling informs Doyle there was no double exposure and that the fairies in the first photo *moved* when the shutter was snapped. He adds that he will stake his reputation on his conclusions. So far things are looking very good, so Doyle trots off to the Kodak Company. Two experts there examine the photographs and admit they can't find evidence of a trick. But there is trouble in pixie paradise.

>> Punch, Counterpunch

The Kodak experts tell Doyle that if they spent a little time on it, they could probably produce similar pictures. Doyle snorts. So now, he says, the character of these little girls is being questioned! You

TRICKS OF THE TRADE

Producing a fake photograph is pretty easy. In fact, in the nineteenth century, legitimate studios did it all the time. The most popular technique involved posing the subject in front of a scenic backdrop. These painted scenes were sold by the square foot from rolls. Props such as columns, chairs, and bookcases gave these composite pictures, as they were called, some depth.

A Kodak camera sold in 1888.

9

can't find anything wrong with the photographs, so you are suggesting that just because you could create a phony picture, these children must have faked something! Harumph! he says, or words to that effect.

Meanwhile, other skeptics want to know why Frances is looking directly at the camera in the first photo and *not at the fairies.* You'd think something as wondrous as a small, winged being would have captured her attention. But Gardner counters that argument. She's seen fairies dozens of times, he replies, but a camera! Now that's really unusual!

The skeptics push forward. "You claim these girls don't have the skill to fake the pictures. Well, we happen to know Elsie worked in a photographer's shop!"

"So what?" Gardner snaps. "She was just an errand girl!"

It goes on like this for a while. Finally, Doyle announces he is heading off to Australia to take in a few séances. Before he leaves, he asks Gardner to get the girls to produce more fairy pictures. Gardner promises he will try.

"My dear Sir Arthur," Gardner writes to Doyle a short while later, "great news! The girls have produced three more wonderful prints!"

Snelling again examines the photographs and once again proclaims the pictures genuine. "Utterly beyond any possibility of faking!" he says, and Gardner declares the case proved. Doyle is now thoroughly convinced that fairies exist. He fires off an article to the *Strand Magazine* titled, "Fairies Photographed—An Epoch-Making Event." This brings reporters to the scene. With notebooks open and pencils poised, they begin to interview Elsie and Frances. "Where did the fairies come from?" they ask. The girls begin to giggle. "We can't say."

The photo of a fairy offering a flower to Elsie *(below)* is the worst of this bunch because the fairy looks so flat and two-dimensional—which, of course, it was.

"Okay. Then, where did the fairies go after you photographed them?" But Elsie and Frances won't talk about that either. The reporters press but to no avail. The girls refuse to discuss the matter further.

The reporters point out that the girls' behavior is extremely suspicious, but Doyle doesn't seem to notice it and dies in 1930 firmly believing in fairies. Had it all been a hoax? No doubt about it. The girls, in fact, eventually confessed, although when they finally came clean, they were well past middle age. But despite the less-than-forceful protests of a few skeptics, a lot of people had been deceived by the fake photos. How did the game go on for so long?

>> Paper, Scissors, Pins

Doyle was hugely popular. The public loved Sherlock Holmes's icy genius and logical mind. So if the pictures were good enough for the greatest detective of all time, well, they must be the real thing. But Doyle was not Sherlock Holmes. He was merely the *author* of Sherlock Holmes. In fact,

Scottish author Sir Arthur Conan Doyle. The analytical and highly skeptical Sherlock Holmes would have been disappointed in his gullible creator.

if anything, he was probably more like the rather dull-witted Dr. Watson. (Doyle had earned his medical degree but turned to writing when his practice floundered.) Doyle's skill lay in creating plots, not in solving real mysteries. Doyle was also very gullible. He had allowed himself to be taken in by spirit mediums, and if he was willing to accept visiting ghosts, why not pixies and gnomes?

Being a theosophist, Edward Gardner already embraced a lot of claptrap, so fooling him was a cinch. And as far as the experts are concerned, some did say the pictures were suspect from the very beginning. Snelling put his seal of approval on them, but he wasn't an expert at spotting faked photographs. He was a professional photographer, and the two are not the same at all.

To make matters even worse, nobody was given the correct information about the pictures. For example, Gardner said the shutter speed was 1/50th of a second, but it was probably closer to two seconds or the image wouldn't have registered. Photographic plates needed fairly long exposure times. And if the shutter was open for two seconds and the fairies were moving, their image would have been a blur.

Another example of incorrect information being passed along has to do with the lighting. The first picture was supposedly taken in full sunlight, but Frances's face is clearly in shadow. Knowing the lighting, the distance between the camera and subject, the type of film used, and so on is important when you are trying to determine if a picture has been faked.

Many years after Doyle and company were hoodwinked, William Spaulding ran a computer analysis on the five fairy photographs. (The analysis was similar to the treatment given to suspicious UFO photos.) Basically, what the computer did was compare the known human figures—Elsie and Frances—to the fairy figures to see if they have the same three-dimensionality. It was hardly a surprise to learn that the fairies were only two-dimensional. In other words, they weren't real beings. What, then, were they?

Below is an illustration for a poem by Alfred Noyes titled, "A Spell for a Fairy." The poem appeared in *Princess Mary's Gift Book,* published in 1915. Do these little fairies look curiously familiar to you?

Dancing fairies from *Princess Mary's Gift Book* inspired Elsie and Frances.

Elsie (*left*), said her mother in 1920, "was a most imaginative child, who has been in the habit of drawing fairies for years." What more can we say?

We now make scissors, wire, and hatpins available to the playful and somewhat mischievous Elsie Wright and Frances Griffiths. We give the girls a camera, one that they know how to use with some degree of skill. We leave them alone for a while. A spirited imagination does the rest, and the gullible are invited to enjoy the results.

CHAPTER 2
GIANTS IN THE EARTH

Our next story made headlines. It actually began in 1866, but we will jump ahead to 1869. That's when the real fun started.

Stub Newell, a farmer in upstate New York, has hired some men to dig a well behind his barn. It is a bright, crisp day in early autumn, and the men are making good progress. Suddenly, one of the shovels clangs loudly.

"Sounds like you hit a rock."

"Pretty likely."

The men continue to dig and quickly realize that the object they have uncovered is no ordinary rock. It is a human being. A very big human being. Wow! Maybe not a human being at all! A giant, 10 feet tall at least. And it's petrified—turned completely to stone! The show is on.

>> Step Right Up, Ladies and Gentlemen . . .

In the small town of Cardiff, word of the giant spreads like butter on a hot flapjack. Newell's neighbors flock to the farm. Then the press shows up. Newell erects a tent over his giant and starts charging half a dollar for a 15-minute look. One after another, they come, they pay, they gawk. Newell is cleaning up. On Sunday, he clears a cool $1,300.

The Cardiff giant, more than 10 feet in length and weighing more than one ton, was discovered buried in the ground in Cardiff, New York, in 1869.

The Cardiff giant became an overnight sensation, drawing crowds from all over the United States to view the find.

"What is it?" the spectators whisper, awed by the giant's imposing frame.

"He must have been in the ground a mighty long time. Look there at how stained that stone is."

The crowd leans forward. Yes, they can see the stains.

"I feel," breathes one man, "that I'm in the presence of a great and superior being." A woman beside him nods respectfully.

"There were giants in the earth in those days," someone mumbles, and the crowd is hushed.

Could this be a member of the race of giants that the Bible talks about in Genesis? Wow! What a find that would be! It would mean all the legends are true!

The scientific community quickly learns of the Cardiff giant. Some of the esteemed scientists rub their beards and nod. They are convinced that a body can be turned into stone if the conditions are right. Others rub their beards and shake their heads. "This is not," they say, "a human being at all, but a statue. Very ancient, no doubt." And still others, like Andrew White of Cornell University, don't rub their beards at all. "Poppycock!" they shout. "The thing's fake!"

Local newspapers in Cardiff and surrounding villages are in love and cover the story with great energy. No need to check out the facts, they all decide. Cardiff is booming. Business is great. But out-of-town newspapers are determined to dig up the truth.

>> A Scheme Hatches

Our story now flashes back three years. George Hull, cigar maker and scoundrel, is looking for a moneymaking scheme. A conversation with a traveling preacher gives him an idea. Two years later, on June 5, 1868, he travels to Fort Dodge, Iowa, where he knows there are gypsum quarries. He hires a man to cut out a 12-foot by 4-foot block, 22 inches thick. Hull then ships the stone block to Chicago. There, two sculptors he has hired carve the block into the shape of a man. Hull knows his petrified man has to look real, so he attaches long, thick

George Hull is pictured here with his creation.

needles to a block of wood and pounds the sculpture to give it pores. He ages it with wet sand, ink, and sulfuric acid. As he stands back to take a look at his handiwork, the smile of a con man plays across his lips. Ahhh, perfect!

Hull has a cousin in upstate New York, Stub Newell. He knows good old Stub will go along with his little hoax, especially since there will be money in it for him. So Hull ships the stone giant east by rail and then hauls it the last few miles by wagon under the cover of night. Two weeks after it arrives, Hull and Newell bury the giant behind Newell's barn. A year later, its discovery explodes across the front pages of newspapers all around the country.

Two weeks into the hoax, Hull decides it's time to get out. He sells three-quarters of his stake in the giant to a group of businessmen for $30,000 and heads off into the sunset. By now, the Cardiff giant has been exposed as the Cardiff fake, but the public doesn't care. The giant goes on a whirlwind tour,

THE GREAT
CARDIFF GIANT!
Discovered at Cardiff, Onondaga Co., N. Y., is now on Exhibition in the
Geological Hall, Albany,
For a few days only.

HIS DIMENSIONS.

Length of Body,	10 feet, 4 1-2 inches.
Length of Head from Chin to Top of Head,	21 "
Length of Nose,	6 "
Across the Nostrils,	3 1-2 "
Width of Mouth,	5 "
Circumference of Neck,	37 "
Shoulders, from point to point,	3 feet, 1 1-2 "
Length of Right Arm,	4 feet, 9 1-2 "
Across the Wrist,	5 "
Across the Palm of Hand,	7 "
Length of Second Finger,	8 "
Around the Thighs,	6 feet, 3 1-2 "
Diameter of the Thigh,	13 "
Through the Calf of Leg,	9 1-2 "
Length of Foot,	21 "
Across the Ball of Foot,	8 "
Weight,	2990 pounds.

ALBANY, November 29th, 1869.

The Cardiff giant appeared "for a few days only" at Geological Hall in Albany, New York. The hoax became a great moneymaker for its perpetrator.

finally landing in the Farmers' Museum in Cooperstown, New York. And as for Hull . . . ?

It is early fall 1877. William Conant and his son are walking just outside the village of Beulah, Colorado, when they notice something strange sticking out of the ground. They kneel down, scrape away some of the soil, and realize it is a man's foot. Further digging reveals a stony, 7½-foot, humanlike creature with a small head and exceptionally long arms. Newspapers rush to the scene. Could this be, they ask breathlessly, the missing link between humans and apes that scientists have been searching for?

Or could it be one more go-around for Mr. George Hull?

Never give a sucker an even break.

CHAPTER 3
RAIN FOREST SHADINESS

Our third story takes place in the jungle. It has everything you could ever want—suffocating humidity, poisonous snakes, mosquitoes the size of airplanes, and a lost tribe of primitive people. The story begins in 1971.

"Come closer," says the man who calls himself Dafal. His dark eyes twinkle with a secret. He is a member of the Blit Manubo tribe on Mindanao, one of the islands that makes up the country called the Philippines. He knows many things.

Manuel Elizalde Jr. leans forward, curious and alert.

(facing page) intriguing photographs of the Tasaday, such as this one taken in April 1972, revealed a primitive people living in the jungles of the Philippines. Their discovery drew interest from anthropologists around the world.

"Not far away," Dafal says, pointing off into the trees, "there is a tribe. Very small. Very primitive. The people live in caves. They have no agriculture and no weapons. They have no domesticated animals. They use only the simplest tools." Dafal spreads his fingers. They are long and graceful. "These people," he continues, "have lived this way for centuries, hidden from the world. No one but me knows they are there. But you, Elizalde, now you know."

Well, Elizalde is not about to sit on this. He zooms back to Manila and hands the story over to the newspapers. And before anyone knows what's happening, the country is crawling with anthropologists. One after the other, they make their way into the steamy Mindanao rain forest. Local guides are more than happy to show them the way to the little lost tribe. The anthropologists gape. They gawk. They take pictures and notes. "This is amazing!" they all say. "These people are still in the Stone Age."

The Tasaday, as the tribe is called, wear loincloths and skirts made of orchid leaves. They have only scrapers, axes, digging sticks, and drills for making fire. They subsist on whatever they can find in the forest—palm fruit, wild bananas, wild yams, crabs, small fish, grubs, and frogs. They have lived this way for centuries, isolated and primitive, a group of 26 people suspended in time. The anthropologists have to pinch themselves. They can't believe it.

>> Paleohippies Meet the World

Within days, it seems, there is a whip-whip-whip of helicopter blades. The churning air shakes the trees and sends dirt and stones scattering. Heads tilt skyward to watch the strange craft touch down on Mindanao. Even before the blades settle to stillness, the door opens, and out jumps a team from *National Geographic* magazine, clad in khakis and weighted down with camera equipment.

When the pictures appear in *National Geographic*'s August 1972 issue, they seem like stills from a movie. Nearly naked people sit, as if posed, on rocky outcroppings. Their soft, brown faces stare blankly at the camera, their lives rudely invaded. *Who are you?* they seem to be saying. We are the world.

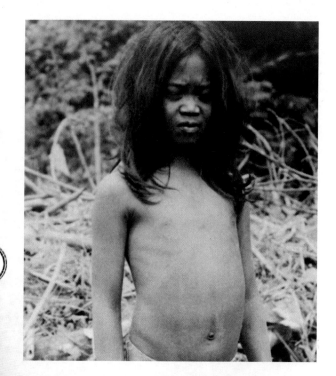

A Tasaday boy

The *National Geographic* story is spellbinding. Readers are enchanted by the simplicity and serenity of the Tasaday. One anthropologist playfully calls them "paleohippies." Everyone has adopted them, and NBC gives Elizalde $50,000 to make a documentary about them. Scholars begin to study their language. Others write books. And

Two of the original Tasaday, Lolo and Bilengan *(left and center)*, were photographed with Datu' Galang *(right)*, a Tboli leader, 1999.

then, just like that, the whole dizzying Tasaday roller coaster screeches to a halt. On September 21, 1972, a corrupt President Ferdinand Marcos declares martial law, and the Philippines suddenly becomes off limits to foreigners. The anthropologists all get whiplash.

For 14 years, nothing is heard from or about the Tasaday. As suddenly as they appeared, they vanished. But in 1986, Marcos is thrown out of power. There is a new government. The Philippines is once again lush and openhearted. Anxious for another close-up look at the Tasaday, Swiss journalist Oswald Iten returns to Mindanao. He hikes through the rain forest, slashing at the overgrowth with a machete. But when he reaches the forest caves, he finds them empty. Hello? Anybody home?

>> You Can't Hide Much in a Pair of Shorts

A shocked Iten does a little poking around and discovers the shy, primitive, Stone Age Tasaday walking around in shorts and T-shirts. They have blended in with Blit Manubo and Tboli tribes and are growing crops, living in huts, and sleeping on wooden beds! Well, Iten knows a scam when

Experts had questioned how the rain forest, which doesn't produce much food fit for humans, could have supported people who didn't rely also on agriculture.

he sees one and announces to the Tasaday that the jig is up. "Come clean," he says. "What goes on here?"

With a little coaxing, a few of the Tasaday confess that the whole thing had been Elizalde's idea. He had asked them to pretend they were a long-lost primitive tribe.

Why? Iten wants to know.

The actors shrug. They don't know. Maybe to fool people. Just for fun. But the only people having fun would have been Elizalde and the Marcos government. Their plan was to give the world an intriguing mystery that would quickly line their pockets. Deep in the heart of the Philippine jungle, they told everyone, a small group of people remains frozen in time. The cave dwellers are from another age, so far away that there are no memories of it. They speak their own language and know nothing of the world that has grown up around them. They are strange and exotic, a lost tribe, just like in the movies. And upon hearing this, the anthropologists would descend like flies. Soon there would be TV coverage, publicity, money! The Philippine government would take over the "Tasaday" forestlands and eventually turn them into private profits for the already bloated Marcos regime. It was the perfect scheme.

But, of course, it wasn't. Several anthropologists had already begun to suspect that something was just not right about the Tasaday. How had such a small group of individuals survived for so long? Why hadn't they died out? The anthropologists also questioned the Tasaday's food source, which was essentially the rain forest itself. Despite how lush it appears, the rain forest would not provide enough food to adequately nourish a human being. All the other tribes who live on Mindanao supplement their diet with crops that they grow.

So when all was said and done, nobody really had much fun after all. President Marcos died in exile, Elizalde never made the piles of money he had hoped for, and the anthropologists went home with nothing except mosquito bites. But maybe the Tasaday had a good time. Everybody wants to be in show biz.

CHAPTER 4
THE *SUN*, THE MOON, AND BATMAN

And now for a little science fiction.

It is August 1835, and so far there are only seven known planets in the solar system. Still, astronomy is making progress. Telescopes are getting bigger and producing sharper images, and scientists are finding things

they never dreamed existed. And life, they believe, is every-
where. No one has proved this yet, of course, but it makes perfect sense. How can Earth be the only inhabited planet in such a
vast universe? The British astronomer Sir William Herschel has
come out in favor of life on the Moon, the planets, and possibly
even the Sun. Others echo his confidence. The time is ripe for a
dandy hoax.

>> The Pen Is Mightier than the Truth

Enter, now, our hero—or perhaps, our villain, depending on your point
of view. He is Richard Locke, ace reporter for the *Sun*, a penny paper in
New York City. When Locke joins the staff, the two-year-old *Sun* is strug-
gling to survive in a field of older, more established
newspapers. Locke knows that if the *Sun* folds, he's out
of a job. So he decides that what the
paper needs is a
really hot story
that will boost
readership and
keep him eating
three squares a day.

The *Sun* breaks the story
about life on the Moon.

Locke pitches his hot story idea to his publisher. The publisher gives him the go-ahead. "Sure, try it," he murmurs. So Locke puts on his thinking cap. Well, in no time at all, Locke is seized with a brainstorm. His eyes twinkle mischievously. "Oooo," he says, or words to that effect. Grinning, he sits down at his desk, dunks his pen into an inkpot, and goes to work.

It is early morning on August 25. An orange midsummer sun rises out of the waters of the East River. The city's newspapers hit the streets with a thwack. The *Sun* hits the streets and leaves a crater. A banner headline shrieks the news: LIFE DISCOVERED ON MOON! The *Sun* completely sells out.

The basis for this remarkable story is supposedly the secretly obtained results of Sir John Herschel's expedition to the

According to Richard Locke, astronomer Sir John Herschel (*right*) described in great detail what he observed as life on the Moon.

An artist rendered this illustration of the Moon based on Locke's accounts in the *Sun*.

Cape of Good Hope, at the foot of Africa. Sir John, son of Sir William and also an astronomer, has gone off to catalog stars in the Southern Hemisphere. But according to the *Sun,* he has also been looking at the Moon and planets though a gigantic telescope he has built. And what do you think he's seen? Why, a lush and lively Moon, that's what! There are forests up there and deep rivers and smooth, sandy beaches. But most extraordinary of all, the *Sun* reports, are the Moon's creatures. In his most flowing style, Locke enthusiastically describes "herds of brown quadrupeds" and gunmetal blue antelopes. There are also unicorns and humanlike beavers, which have discovered fire and live in nicely constructed huts.

The *Sun*'s readers are breathless. Naturally they want more, so Locke bangs out Part 2 of the story. It's published the following day. Locke is really cooking now. His clever mixture of fact, fantasy, and seasoned newspaper savvy is selling papers so fast, the presses can hardly keep up. By the third installment, readers are practically drooling. Letters pour into the *Sun*'s offices. Everyone wants to know if there are people on the Moon. Readership is soaring. No one else is carrying the story. (And you know why.) It's the greatest scoop of all time! The publisher of the *Sun* is dancing on the desks. "Go ahead!" he shouts gleefully to Locke. "Tell 'em about the Moon people!"

>> All This and Batman Too.

In the fourth installment, Locke delivers the goods. The Moon, he reveals to thousands of panting readers, is inhabited by man-bats. Their scientific name is *Verspertilio homo.* The man-bats are four feet high and covered

The *Sun* wowed its readers with reports of man-bats living on the Moon.

with short, reddish hair. Their huge wings extend from the top of their shoulders to their calves, and when not walking upright, they soar effortlessly through the fragrant lunar air. Their faces resemble that of the orangutan, but they are very humanlike in their expressions. (All this Herschel is supposedly seeing through a telescope.)

August melts into September, and the installments keep coming. Newspapers up and down the East Coast actually applaud the *Sun*'s handling of the story. Even the *New York Times* is impressed and calls the reports "probable and plausible." But wait. It gets even wackier.

One afternoon, Locke looks up from his desk and sees two gentlemen.

"Mr. Locke?"

Our hero nods.

"I am Professor Dennison Olmstead and this is my colleague Professor Elias Loomis. We're from Yale University."

Locke knows what's coming but remains composed. He politely extends his hand. Everyone shakes.

"We are most anxious," says Olmstead, "to have a look at those lunar calculations."

"Uh, yes," says Locke. He pushes out a smile.

The *Sun*, it seems, has been telling its readers that it has proof of all the lunacy it's been dishing out. There are supposedly 40 pages of mathematical computations from the *Edinburgh Journal of Science* that show how all this Moon life could have developed.

Getting Your Money's Worth

In the early nineteenth century, newspapers were as dull as dishwater, dealing only with political and financial news. Then came Benjamin Day, a New York City printer. In 1833, Day published the first edition of the *New York Sun*, a four-page penny paper. Day believed in giving the public what they wanted—humor, entertainment, and lots of crime and violence. The *Sun* was an instant hit. Other penny papers tried to match Day's success, and the race was on to find—or make up— the most lurid and sensational stories.

Eventually, most of the penny papers folded. The *Sun*, however, kept going even after Day sold it in 1868. It continued to sell well, but the stories gradually grew more conservative. In 1916, the *Sun* merged with the *New York Press* and, a few years later, the *Globe*. By 1950 it was all but gone, surviving as only the last two words on the front page of the *New York World-Telegram and Sun*. And eventually that, too, folded.

The *Sun* didn't print any of it because it was much too technical for the average reader. *But these two guys,* Locke is now thinking, *are not the average reader. They're scientists. Hmmm. Now what?*

Locke swallows. "Well, Professors," he says. "A funny thing. The papers are not here. If you can believe it, we sent them off to the printer not 10 minutes ago. Down the hall, turn left, take the stairs two flights, down the hall, turn right." He adds another smile.

Off go the professors. But the printer also has bad news. "You just missed them," he says. "The papers were shipped out."

The professors are again on the move, and by day's end, they have toured half of New York with nothing to show for it. If they are starting to get suspicious, they keep it to themselves.

By September, Locke decides he's had enough. One of his friends at the *Journal of Commerce* is just about to reprint the story, and Locke finds he doesn't have the heart to let the guy go through with it. He confesses all, and the *Journal* gets a scoop on an exposé of the Great Moon Hoax. The *Sun* never apologizes.

"Who cares if we made it all up?" says its publisher. "We sold a few papers and everybody had a good read."

So much for responsible journalism. As for Herschel, well, he thinks the whole thing is pretty funny and admits that his actual discoveries probably won't be half as interesting. And the public?

Some of us still believe everything we read.

CHAPTER 5

GRAFFITI IN THE GRAIN

Our last story is a good old-fashioned mystery. Naturally, it takes place in England, birthplace of great mysteries. The year is 1965. The place is Warminster in southern England. The night is dark but not stormy. Had there been a storm, Gordon Faulkner wouldn't have been able to get a decent photograph of the disk-shaped UFO. But the night sky is clear, so Gordon gets his snapshot.

The photograph quickly makes its way into the tabloids and triggers a rash of UFO sightings. Everyone in Warminster, it seems, is seeing lights in the sky. Night after night, the people gather atop Cradle Hill and Starr

Hill, the two best viewing sites in town. And the UFOs do not disappoint. The crowd is treated to a variety show of mysterious lights, strange shapes, and eerie sounds. This goes on for quite some time, and Warminster gains the reputation of being UFO Central.

>> UFO Footprints?

We now jump ahead 15 years. It is a quiet day in early August 1980. A tourist has come to see Britain's famous chalk giants. As he walks along the earthworks, his eyes settle on a field at the foot of the hill. There, etched in the grain, are three enormous circles. The tourist blinks and blinks again. "Well, this is certainly quite curious," he thinks. The circles are very precise and perfectly shaped and look, well . . . *wrong* in the middle of the grain. Intrigued by the mystery, the tourist phones the offices of the nearby *Wiltshire Times.* The *Wiltshire Times* is a small

Facing page: A prehistoric chalk horse carved into a hillside in Wiltshire, England. *Below:* An early crop circle, Wiltshire, 1989

weekly newspaper, but it is professional in every respect. A short time later, a reporter and a photographer arrive on the scene. When the paper publishes its next edition a few days later, the eye-catching headline sets the stage.

MYSTERY CIRCLES—RETURN OF THE "THING?"

Despite what it sounds like, the "Thing" is not some mutant reptile that tramples cities. It is, instead, the *Times*'s nickname for the legendary Warminster UFO from the 1960s. Is the paper suggesting that aliens made the circles? Well, not exactly, but the story certainly fires up people's imaginations.

UFO enthusiasts lick their lips. The day after the *Times* article appears, Ian Mrzyglod, Mike Seager, Terry Chivers, and Julie Blake show up in Warminster to investigate. Mrzyglod and his team are amateur researchers, but they have a keen interest in getting at

A crop circle investigator takes measurements and notes in a field.

the truth. They describe themselves as skeptical and well aware that 90 percent of all UFO sightings turn out to be known objects. So armed with measuring tapes, cameras, and plastic bags, the team of four fans out to gather evidence.

One of the circles is in a field of winter wheat on Geoff Cooper's farm. Cooper tells Mrzyglod that this is the *second* one he found. The first circle appeared in May, but it had since been plowed under. The other two circles are on the neighboring Scull farm, pressed into an oat field. Scull says he discovered one on the morning of July 21 and the other 10 days later, also in the morning.

"Did you hear anything? See anything?" Mrzyglod asks. Scull and Cooper shake their heads.

Cooper rubs his chin. "But my housekeeper," he says, "she did. Strange humming sounds, she said they were coming from the fields. They'd be on for 20 minutes, and then off for 10, on for 20, off for 10. The dogs were barking, too. All night long."

>> Theories, Anyone?

Mrzyglod and the others can see that the grain has been flattened—not cut—and that the stalks all lie swirled in a clockwise direction. Mrzyglod suggests four possibilities. The circles were made by a UFO, a helicopter, a hoaxer, or a whirlwind of some kind. The researchers go to work. They send soil and stalk samples from the three sites to a technician at Bristol University, who tests them for radioactivity. (UFO researchers seem to think that a flying saucer landing site should be radioactive.) The report comes back negative. Mrzyglod decides to set aside the UFO hypothesis for lack of any substantial proof.

Researchers were amazed that the stalks in crop circles were bent but not broken. What could have caused such results? they wondered.

Both the British Army and the Royal Aeronautical Society deny that any helicopters were in the area, so that theory goes down. The team also concludes that the circles probably weren't made as a hoax, mostly because nobody can find any trails through the cornstalks. A hoaxer would have had to come in with a machine of some kind and would have certainly trampled the grain. But there's no sign that anything was dragged, lugged, or ridden onto the field. So all that's left is the whirlwind theory.

At first, this one seems like a winner. At Mrzyglod's request, Terence Meaden, an expert on tornadoes and bizarre weather, agrees to study the crop circles. And yes, he concludes, a whirlwind certainly could have created the swirling pattern. He then goes on to describe low-pressure pockets and thermal updrafts. It's all very scientific and all very convincing. Meaden is confident. Mrzyglod and his research team are satisfied. But the game is just getting started.

>> you Can Fool a Lot of the People a Lot of the Time

The following summer, almost to the day, three more crop circles appear at a place called the Devil's Punchbowl at Cheesefoot Head. This time, however, they don't look quite so "natural." They are strung out in a line, with the inner circle almost twice as large as the two outer ones. Meaden, puzzled by the symmetry of the design, adjusts his theory. He adds prevailing winds, leeward slopes, and oncoming frontal systems.

UFO buffs, meanwhile, are convinced the circles are flying saucer landing sites, called "nests." When the spinning disk lifts off (supposedly), circulating air flattens the grain, leaving behind a depression that resembles a bird's nest. And if ever there was a spot for UFO nests, this part of England is certainly it!

Crop circles continued to show up in England throughout the 1980s and 1990s.

Some crop circles have very intricate patterns, such as this one that appeared in Wiltshire, England, in 1990.

Baffled and intrigued, curious and delighted, one and all they flock to the crop circles. They measure them. They photograph them. They test the soil and study the crushed stalks under microscopes. The UFO buffs set up viewing areas to watch for flying saucer activity. The skeptics rig night vision cameras in the hope of catching the sneaky circle makers in the act. But everyone is outfoxed. Summer after summer, the circles continue to appear wherever the watchers aren't. The patterns are now very stylized, and some are even starting to resemble occult symbols. "They're messages!" breathe the UFO nuts, "from *out there!*"

Thirteen years pass.

Insectograms are crop circles in the form of giant insects, such as this antlike crop circle in Hampshire, England.

"Well," Dave Chorley may have said, one late summer afternoon, "I think I've had enough."

Doug Bower would then have nodded. "Yes. We're too old for this."

"It was fun, though, wasn't it?"

"Our best prank, I'd say."

"I thought they'd get it after we made the insectograms."

"Pretty foolish, they were."

And Doug may have chuckled softly at the public's willingness to believe all kinds of nonsense.

So it came to pass that on the morning of September 4, Dave Chorley and Doug Bower formally confessed to a reporter. With a

Dave Chorely and Doug Bower plot out a crop circle. Dave and Doug were the first to flatten symbols in fields, but they have inspired many other crop artists around the world.

heavy steel bar, and then later with 4-foot-long planks and ropes, they had made the crop circles. In Cheesefoot Head and Warminster. At Wantage and Winterbourne Stoke. At Chilcomb and near Stonehenge. No helicopters, no whirlpools, and no aliens. It had all been done by two practical jokers, now in their 60s, after a few pints of stout at the local pub.

The mystery of the crop circles was finally solved, and everyone should have been happy, except nobody really was. The scientists had been hoodwinked, and that embarrassed them. The people who had invented the new field (no pun intended) of "cereology" watched a source of income turn into a vapor. And the UFO lovers who thought they were finally going to make contact had their hopes dashed. So there was only one thing left to do. Ignore the confession.

Crop circles still show up every now and then. It's a strange ending to the story. But human beings are a funny bunch. We love a good hoax. It shows enterprise and inventiveness. Even if we wind up with egg on our faces, it doesn't matter. It's usually fun while it lasts. And sometimes, it sure beats the truth.

Books// Boese, Alex. *The Museum of Hoaxes: A Collection of Pranks, Stunts, Deceptions, and Other Wonderful Stories Contrived for the Public from the Middle Ages to the New Millennium.* New York: E. P. Dutton, 2002. This book details true stories of frauds and scams, from art forgeries to alien invasions.

Wilker, Josh. *Classic Cons and Swindles.* Broomall, PA: Chelsea House Publishing, 1997. This book takes a look at some of the scams and hoaxes con artists have used to swindle money from unsuspecting people.

Videos// *FairyTale: A True Story.* London: Icon Entertainment International, 1997. This movie about the Cottingley fairies was filmed in Yorkshire, England, where the real Elsie Wright and Frances Griffiths lived. All the characters involved in the original story are featured, including the fairies. Rated PG for brief mild language.

Signs. Los Angeles: Touchstone Pictures, 2002. In this movie, Mel Gibson stars as a farmer who discovers something very strange happening in his cornfield. Rated PG-13 for some scary moments.

Websites// Hoaxes
<http://www.lhup.edu/~dsimanek/hoaxes.htm>
Some of history's most famous scams are examined on this website, run by Dr. Donald E. Simanek, a retired physics professor.

The Museum of Hoaxes
<www.museumofhoaxes.com>
This website includes a frequently updated weblog of scams and practical jokes from around the world. It also features the Top 100 April Fool's gags, a glossary of tall-tale creatures, and a gallery of photographic hoaxes. The website itself contains a few gags, so readers beware.

>> Index

>> About the Author

Born in Baltimore, Maryland, Judith Herbst grew up in Queens, New York, where she learned to jump double Dutch with amazing skill. She has since lost that ability. A former English teacher, she ran away from school in her tenure year to become a writer. Her first book for kids was *Sky Above and Worlds Beyond,* whose title, she admits, was much too long. She loves to write and would rather be published, she says, than be rich, which has turned out to be the case. Herbst spends summers in Maine on a lake with her cats and laptop.

>> Photo Acknowledgments

Photographs and illustrations in this book are used courtesy of: Fortean Picture Library, pp. 7 (both), 11 (all), 12, 14, 15, 36, 37 (Terence Meaden), 38 (Dr. G. T. Meaden), 40 (Bob Skinner), 41 (Bob Skinner), 42, 44 (Robert Irving); © Bettmann/CORBIS, pp. 9, 17, 18, 19, 20, 22, 24, 31, 32; © Robin Hemley, p. 25; © Stephen G. Donaldson Photography, p. 26; © AIP Emilio Segré Visual Archives, T. J. J. See Collection, p. 30; © Christopher Cormack/CORBIS, p. 43. Illustrations by Bill Hauser, pp. 4–5, 6, 16, 28, 29.

Cover photograph by © Christopher Cormack/CORBIS